FILL THIS SPAC

Copyright © 2018 by Adam J. Kurtz

All rights reserved. This book (or any portion thereof) may not be reproduced or used in any manner without the express written permission of the publisher except for the use of brief quotations in book reviews or coverage.

First Printing: 2018

ISBN: 9-780996907-248

ADAMJK Press
P.O. Box 550
Brooklyn, NY 11211

www.adamjk.com
◎ 🐦 adamjk

UNSOLICITED ADVICE
2019 WEEKLY PLANNER
BY ADAM J. KURTZ

HELLO!

LET'S JUST GET THE SCARY ~~SHIT~~ OUT OF THE WAY NOW: LIFE IS HARD. LIFE IS FULL OF BAD NEWS HAPPENING TO US PERSONALLY, TO THOSE WE LOVE & OTHERS WE DON'T EVEN KNOW.

BUT GOOD THINGS HAPPEN. LOVE IS REAL. WE WILL BE OK.

DESPITE THE DARK PARTS, LIFE IS FULL OF AMAZING MOMENTS. SOME OF THEM WE EVEN GET TO EXPERIENCE.

YOU WERE BORN (WITHOUT YOUR EXPRESS PERMISSION BUT WHATEVER). THAT'S A DAY TO CELEBRATE. SPECIAL ANNIVERSARIES. PLANS WITH FRIENDS. IT'S ALL HERE.

AGAIN (SORRY), LIFE CAN BE BAD (STILL SORRY). BUT SO MANY GREAT THINGS ARE TO COME. LIFE GETS BETTER WHEN WE LIVE IT TOGETHER. SO HERE WE ARE. ME (A STRANGER WHO WROTE THIS PLANNER) & YOU (A VERY NICE PERSON PROBABLY). WE'RE GONNA DO OUR BEST.

FLIP AHEAD & MARK THE DAYS THAT ARE SPECIAL TO YOU!! I'VE GONE THROUGH TO NOTE ALL THOSE QUESTIONABLY-REAL NONSENSE HOLIDAYS. I ADDED DISTRACTIONS & ENCOURAGEMENT & YES, UNSOLICITED ADVICE.

LIFE IS HARD BUT MOSTLY WORTH IT. THANKS FOR BEING HERE.

—Adam

2019 OVERVIEW

Here goes nothing??? There are a lot of ways to look at a year. Below, monthly grids you can cross out or count down on. To the right, a tracking grid for your progress, period, or anything else you want to stay on top of. Let's do this!

JANUARY

S	M	T	W	T	F	S
		1	2	3	4	5
6	7	8	9	10	11	12
13	14	15	16	17	18	19
20	21	22	23	24	25	26
27	28	29	30	31		

FEBRUARY

S	M	T	W	T	F	S
					1	2
3	4	5	6	7	8	9
10	11	12	13	14	15	16
17	18	19	20	21	22	23
24	25	26	27	28		

MARCH

S	M	T	W	T	F	S
					1	2
3	4	5	6	7	8	9
10	11	12	13	14	15	16
17	18	19	20	21	22	23
24	25	26	27	28	29	30
31						

APRIL

S	M	T	W	T	F	S
	1	2	3	4	5	6
7	8	9	10	11	12	13
14	15	16	17	18	19	20
21	22	23	24	25	26	27
28	29	30				

MAY

S	M	T	W	T	F	S
			1	2	3	4
5	6	7	8	9	10	11
12	13	14	15	16	17	18
19	20	21	22	23	24	25
26	27	28	29	30	31	

JUNE

S	M	T	W	T	F	S
						1
2	3	4	5	6	7	8
9	10	11	12	13	14	15
16	17	18	19	20	21	22
23	24	25	26	27	28	29
30						

JULY

S	M	T	W	T	F	S
	1	2	3	4	5	6
7	8	9	10	11	12	13
14	15	16	17	18	19	20
21	22	23	24	25	26	27
28	29	30	31			

AUGUST

S	M	T	W	T	F	S
				1	2	3
4	5	6	7	8	9	10
11	12	13	14	15	16	17
18	19	20	21	22	23	24
25	26	27	28	29	30	31

SEPTEMBER

S	M	T	W	T	F	S
1	2	3	4	5	6	7
8	9	10	11	12	13	14
15	16	17	18	19	20	21
22	23	24	25	26	27	28
29	30					

OCTOBER

S	M	T	W	T	F	S
		1	2	3	4	5
6	7	8	9	10	11	12
13	14	15	16	17	18	19
20	21	22	23	24	25	26
27	28	29	30	31		

NOVEMBER

S	M	T	W	T	F	S
					1	2
3	4	5	6	7	8	9
10	11	12	13	14	15	16
17	18	19	20	21	22	23
24	25	26	27	28	29	30

DECEMBER

S	M	T	W	T	F	S
1	2	3	4	5	6	7
8	9	10	11	12	13	14
15	16	17	18	19	20	21
22	23	24	25	26	27	28
29	30	31				

SUN	MON	TUE	WED	THU	FRI	SAT	SUN	MON	TUE	WED	THU	FRI	SAT
		1 JAN	2	3	4	5	6	7	8	9	10	11	12
13	14	15	16	17	18	19	20	21	22	23	24	25	26
27	28	29	30	31	1 FEB	2	3	4	5	6	7	8	9
10	11	12	13	14	15	16	17	18	19	20	21	22	23
24	25	26	27	28	1 MAR	2	3	4	5	6	7	8	9
10	11	12	13	14	15	16	17	18	19	20	21	22	23
24	25	26	27	28	29	30	31	1 APR	2	3	4	5	6
7	8	9	10	11	12	13	14	15	16	17	18	19	20
21	22	23	24	25	26	27	28	29	30	1 MAY	2	3	4
5	6	7	8	9	10	11	12	13	14	15	16	17	18
19	20	21	22	23	24	25	26	27	28	29	30	31	1 JUN
2	3	4	5	6	7	8	9	10	11	12	13	14	15
16	17	18	19	20	21	22	23	24	25	26	27	28	29
30	1 JUL	2	3	4	5	6	7	8	9	10	11	12	13
14	15	16	17	18	19	20	21	22	23	24	25	26	27
28	29	30	31	1 AUG	2	3	4	5	6	7	8	9	10
11	12	13	14	15	16	17	18	19	20	21	22	23	24
25	26	27	28	29	30	31	1 SEP	2	3	4	5	6	7
8	9	10	11	12	13	14	15	16	17	18	19	20	21
22	23	24	25	26	27	28	29	30	1 OCT	2	3	4	5
6	7	8	9	10	11	12	13	14	15	16	17	18	19
20	21	22	23	24	25	26	27	28	29	30	31	1 NOV	2
3	4	5	6	7	8	9	10	11	12	13	14	15	16
17	18	19	20	21	22	23	24	25	26	27	28	29	30
1 DEC	2	3	4	5	6	7	8	9	10	11	12	13	14
15	16	17	18	19	20	21	22	23	24	25	26	27	28
29	30	31											

2018 REFLECTIONS

Take some time to look back at the year you had. What accomplishments, moments or experiences feel the most significant to you? What do you hope to leave in the past? Can you identify a single fundamental lesson that the year taught you?

2014 PROJECTIONS

It's a whole new year of your life! While lots of things remain the same many things will change. It's not all in our control but a lot of it is, so take some time to think about where you'll be and what you want to accomplish.

EMERGENCY CONTACTS

Paper address books are pretty much not a thing anymore, which makes sense. We have all the numbers! So many numbers! But what happens when you're actually in an "emergency" and you don't know WHO to call? That's what this page is for.

Nicest person I know:

Dad:

Kindest person I know:

Other Dad:

Mom:

Perfect date spot but need to call ahead:

Basically my mom:

Senator I gotta keep calling to hold accountable:

Owes me a favor:

Sibling that I love the most:

Owed a favor:

Sibling that I love but don't really like right now:

Really good American-style Chinese delivery:

National Suicide Prevention Lifeline:

1-800-273-8255

Really good actual Chinese food:

Therapist phone number:

Person who knows everything:

Personal mentor (whether they know it or not):

Friend I can always talk to:

Love of my life (ok to leave blank for now):

Person I cannot talk to DO NOT PICK UP:

Pizza (delivery apps charge businesses ~20% btw):

GROWN-UP CHORE CHART

If you ever had a "chore chart" growing up, you already know. Give yourself a little extra encouragement by rewarding stars, smiley faces, or anything else in the boxes below each time you accomplish each task.

Went to the gym or engaged in some other form of physical activity without Instagramming it					
Tried tucking in your shirt and it actually looked good and not like you are an adult toddler					
Mailed rent check on time despite it being 2019 and nobody else uses checks for anything else					
Somehow made a new friend despite it being so hard to make new friends????? But you did it!!!					
Registered to vote, actually voted, made your friends register to vote, went with them to vote					
Unfollowed someone online who you can't stop comparing yourself to for some reason					
Noticed that somebody unfollowed you and didn't immediately question your whole life					
Liked an album so much that you literally paid money to the artist who made it for their work					
Called a family member just to say hi and it's not even their birthday you just wanted to say hi					
Treated someone to lunch even if it's not fancy it's just a nice gesture people appreciate it					
Made an effort to relax and calm down before bringing that energy into someone else's space					
Took a long shower that's a little too hot and let all the water pour on your stupid head but it's ok					
Left a surprisingly large tip for special meal that you enjoyed to pass that celebration along					

"ZZAH BRAHS" PIZZA RATINGS

Pizza is without a doubt the ultimate food – it's cheap, it's delicious, and it's readily available almost everywhere. Rank the slices and track the places you enjoy this year.

0/8 — Nah, Brah

IF YOU'RE BUYIN'

4/8 — Well, it's pizza

CHEESUS CRUST!

8/8 — Slice of Heaven

Restaurant Name

Restaurant Name

Restaurant Name

Restaurant Name

Restaurant Name

Restaurant Name

Restaurant Name

Restaurant Name

Restaurant Name

Restaurant Name

INSTANT GRAMS

People–including you–are leading highly curated lives on social media. That doesn't mean these aren't honest experiences, but there's still a lot of pressure to "do things" and "be places" daily. Here are some backups to save to your drafts just in case.

- DEFINITELY AN AD??? I THINK?
- POSITIVITY CONTENT (I'M SAD)
- A VERY GOOD BOY (DOG)
- FIREWORKS (OUT OF FOCUS)
- A NICE ART W/ ARTIST CREDIT
- MEMORY OF A BETTER TIME

New Year's Resolution:

Actually accomplish the goal before telling everyone about it online

> GIVE YOURSELF PERMISSION TO TRY THAT ONE THING YOU'VE BEEN DENYING YOURSELF

PERSONAL GOALS FOR THE MONTH AHEAD:

_____

_____

_____

EXCITING ~~SHIT~~ HAPPENING SOON TO PREPARE FOR:

_____

_____

_____

DON'T FORGET:

_____

_____

THAT THING I DIDN'T ACTUALLY GET DONE:

_____

ONE POSITIVE THOUGHT:

_____

JANUARY

SUNDAY	MONDAY	TUESDAY	WEDNESDAY	THURSDAY	FRIDAY	SATURDAY
		1	2	3	4	5
6	7	8	9	10	11	12
13	14	15	16	17	18	19
20	21	22	23	24	25	26
27	28	29	30	31		

JANUARY

Monday

OH GOD OH NO HERE WE GO!

Tuesday New Year's Day 2019
1

Wednesday
2

Thursday
3

REWARD YOURSELF

Friday
4

ENJOY THE UNKNOWN

Bird Day

Saturday
5

● NEW MOON

Sunday
6

FEELING GOOD ABOUT:	COMING UP NEXT:
NEED TO WORK ON:	

JANUARY

Monday
7

Tuesday   Earth's Rotation Day
8

Wednesday
9

DO SOME GOOD

Thursday   Houseplant Appreciation Day
10

Friday
11

Saturday
12

TRY TRYING

Sunday
13

FEELING GOOD ABOUT:	COMING UP NEXT:
NEED TO WORK ON:	

JANUARY

Monday
14

Feast Of The Ass (Google It)

Tuesday
15

Wednesday
16

CALL A FRIEND

Thursday
17

Friday
18

Good Memory Day

Saturday
19

EMBRACE MORTALITY???

Sunday
20

♒ AQUARIUS SEASON

FEELING GOOD ABOUT:	COMING UP NEXT:
NEED TO WORK ON:	

JANUARY

Monday　　　　　　　　　　　　　　　　Martin Luther King Jr. Day
21

O FULL MOON

Tuesday　　　　　　　　　　　　　　　　Roe Vs. Wade Day
22

Wednesday
23

Thursday
24

TAKE SOME TIME

THANK YOU COME AGAIN

Friday
25

Saturday
26

KNOW THAT YOU DON'T KNOW

Sunday
27

FEELING GOOD ABOUT:

COMING UP NEXT:

NEED TO WORK ON:

JANUARY

Monday   Bubble Wrap Appreciation Day
28

Tuesday
29

Wednesday   National Croissant Day
30

EXPECT GOOD THINGS SOON

Thursday
31

FEBRUARY

SUNDAY	MONDAY	TUESDAY	WEDNESDAY	THURSDAY	FRIDAY	SATURDAY
					1	2
3	4	5	6	7	8	9
10	11	12	13	14	15	16
17	18	19	20	21	22	23
24	25	26	27	28		

PERSONAL GOALS FOR THE MONTH AHEAD:

___

EXCITING ~~SHIT~~ HAPPENING SOON TO PREPARE FOR:

___

DON'T FORGET:

___

THAT THING I DIDN'T ACTUALLY GET DONE:

___

ONE POSITIVE THOUGHT:

___

FEBRUARY

Black History Month · **Friday 1**

Groundhog Day · **Saturday 2**

YOU CAN'T EVER RUN AWAY

Anniversary of Beyonce's Super Bowl Performance · **Sunday 3**

FEELING GOOD ABOUT:

NEED TO WORK ON:

COMING UP NEXT:

FEBRUARY

Monday
4

● NEW MOON

Tuesday　　　　　　　　　　　Chinese New Year (Year of the Pig)
5

BE KIND ALWAYS

Wednesday
6

Thursday
7

Friday
8

National Bagel Day

Saturday
9

BE NICE (MOSTLY)

Sunday
10

FEELING GOOD ABOUT:	COMING UP NEXT:
NEED TO WORK ON:	

FEBRUARY

Monday
11

FOLLOW BACK

GET OUTTA HERE

Tuesday
12

Wednesday   Galentine's Day
13

Thursday   Valentine's Day
14

PUT SOME FEELINGS IN HERE SO YOU CAN IGNORE THEM FOR A WHILE & SEE WHAT HAPPENS

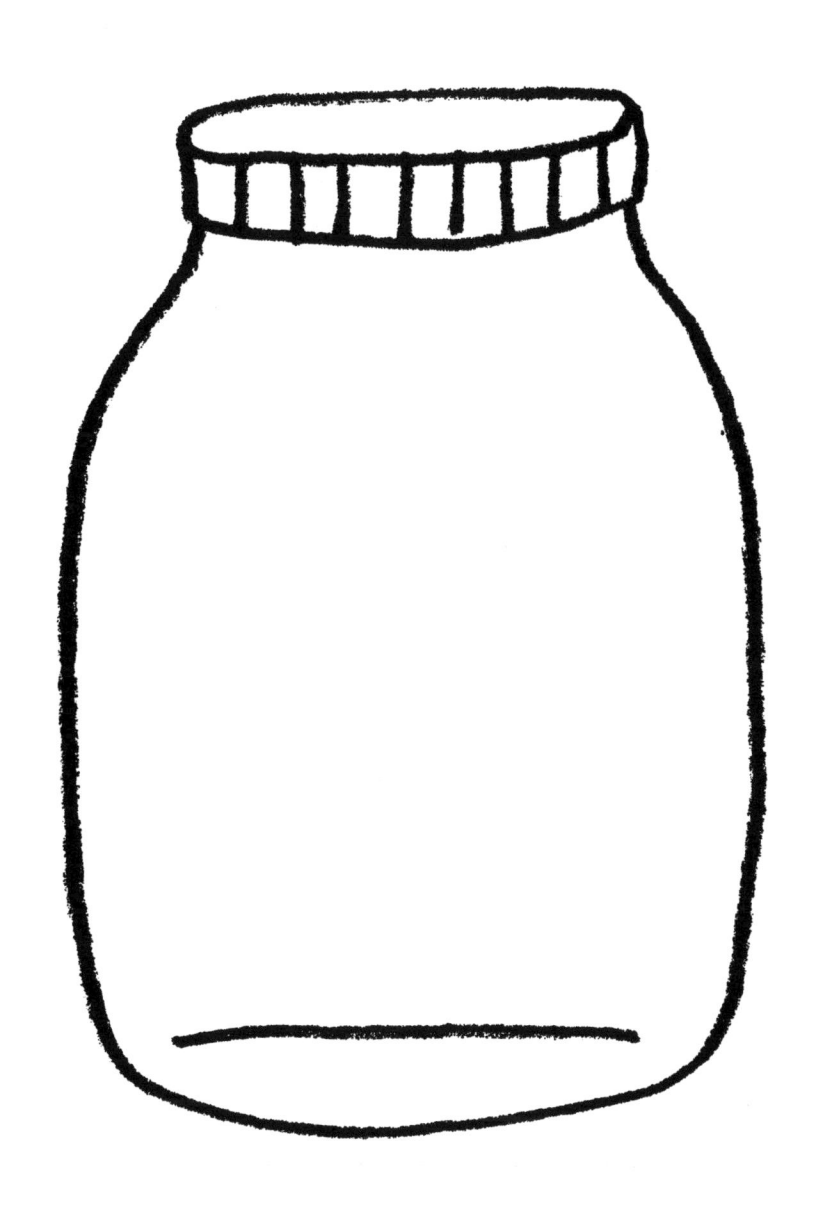

THERE'S ALWAYS ONE REALLY HOT GUY IN THE YOGA CLASS WHO'S GOT LONG HAIR & LEAN MUSCLES & CAN FOLD INTO ANY SHAPE & SEEMS JUST LIKE WAY MORE ENLIGHTENED THAN YOU'LL EVER BE ANYWAY THAT'S MY HUSBAND SO BACK OFF

WRITE SOMETHING WITHOUT THINKING — IT'S OK IF IT'S BAD LITERALLY NOBODY WILL MIND

GOOD THINGS HAPPEN

LOVE IS REAL

WE WILL BE OKAY

FEBRUARY

Friday
15

Do A Grouch A Favor Day

Saturday
16

Sunday
17

TAKE A BATH

FEELING GOOD ABOUT:	COMING UP NEXT:
NEED TO WORK ON:	

FEBRUARY

Monday Presidents' Day
18

Tuesday
19

○ FULL MOON
♓ PISCES SEASON

Wednesday
20

Thursday
21

LEARN SOMETHING NEW

National Margarita Day

Friday
22

Saturday
23

Sunday
24

MAKE A PLAYLIST FOR TONIGHT

FEELING GOOD ABOUT:	COMING UP NEXT:
NEED TO WORK ON:	

FEBRUARY

Monday
25

Tuesday
26

Wednesday   Inconvenience Yourself Day
27

Thursday
28

INHALE, EXHALE

MARCH

SUNDAY	MONDAY	TUESDAY	WEDNESDAY	THURSDAY	FRIDAY	SATURDAY
					1	2
3	4	5	6	7	8	9
10	11	12	13	14	15	16
17	18	19	20	21	22	23
24	25	26	27	28	29	30
30						

PERSONAL GOALS FOR THE MONTH AHEAD:

_____

_____

_____

EXCITING ~~SHIT~~ HAPPENING SOON TO PREPARE FOR:

_____

_____

_____

DON'T FORGET:

_____

_____

THAT THING I DIDN'T ACTUALLY GET DONE:

_____

ONE POSITIVE THOUGHT:

_____

MARCH

Women's History Month
Read Across America Day

Friday
1

A HAPPY END-ING

Saturday
2

DELETE YOUR ACCOUNT

Sunday
3

FEELING GOOD ABOUT:

NEED TO WORK ON:

COMING UP NEXT:

MARCH

Monday
4

NEVER FORGET THAT 1 THING

Tuesday — Mardi Gras
5

☆ MERCURY RETROGRADE BEGINS

Wednesday
6

● NEW MOON

Thursday — National Cereal Day
7

PACK A FUN LUNCH

Friday
8

YOU CAN'T "GET LOST" IF YOU ALREADY ARE

Saturday
9

Daylight Savings Time Starts

Sunday
10

FEELING GOOD ABOUT:

NEED TO WORK ON:

COMING UP NEXT:

MARCH

Monday
11

Tuesday   National Girl Scout Day
12

Wednesday
13

Thursday
14

CREATE ANYTHING REALLY

AH SHIT, SORRY

Friday
15

Saturday
16

St. Patrick's Day (White People Holiday)   **Sunday**
17

BRUSH YOUR HAIR IF YOU HAVE SOME

FEELING GOOD ABOUT:	COMING UP NEXT:
NEED TO WORK ON:	

MARCH

Monday
18

LIFE IS SURPRISING BUT PATTERNS FORM

Tuesday
19

Wednesday   First Day of Spring
20

O FULL MOON

Thursday   World Poetry Day
21

♈ ARIES SEASON

Friday
22

National Puppy Day
OK Day

Saturday
23

Sunday
24

THAT FEELING MIGHT HAVE A POINT

FEELING GOOD ABOUT:	COMING UP NEXT:
NEED TO WORK ON:	

MARCH

Monday
25

Tuesday
26

IT'S OK TO BE OPEN

Wednesday
27

Thursday   Respect Your Cat Day
28

★ MERCURY RETROGRADE ENDS

Friday
29

Pencil Day

Saturday
30

Sunday
31

LOVE IS (WEIRDLY) REAL

FEELING GOOD ABOUT:	COMING UP NEXT:
NEED TO WORK ON:	

APRIL

Monday
1
It's Definitely Not April Fool's Day

Tuesday
2

FOCUS ON THE PEOPLE WHO CARE

Wednesday
3

Thursday
4
National Burrito Day

APRIL

SUNDAY	MONDAY	TUESDAY	WEDNESDAY	THURSDAY	FRIDAY	SATURDAY
	1	2	3	4	5	6
7	8	9	10	11	12	13
14	15	16	17	18	19	20
21	22	23	24	25	26	27
28	29	30				

PERSONAL GOALS FOR THE MONTH AHEAD:

___

EXCITING ~~SHIT~~ HAPPENING SOON TO PREPARE FOR:

___

DON'T FORGET:

___

THAT THING I DIDN'T ACTUALLY GET DONE:

___

ONE POSITIVE THOUGHT:

___

APRIL

Friday
5

● NEW MOON

Saturday
6

IT'S NOT A CONTEST

Sunday
7

FEELING GOOD ABOUT:	COMING UP NEXT:
NEED TO WORK ON:	

APRIL

Monday
8

Tuesday　　　　　　　　　　　　　　　　　　　Name Yourself Day
9

Wednesday
10

THE ANSWERS HAVE QUESTIONS

Thursday
11

Friday
12

TAKE CARE

Saturday
13

National Dolphin Day **Sunday**
14

FEELING GOOD ABOUT:

COMING UP NEXT:

NEED TO WORK ON:

APRIL

Monday
15
                                                                    Tax Day (USA)

Tuesday
16

Wednesday
17

Thursday
18

SELF-CARE ISN'T JUST A TREND

WHAT CAN YOU CREATE WITH ONE PENCIL IN TEN MINUTES?

YOU DO NOT NEED TO JUSTIFY WHY YOU'RE TIRED... BUT YOU DO NEED TO REST.

IT'S OK TO TEAR THIS TO PIECES

ERROR 404:

THIS PAGE LITERALLY CANNOT

APRIL

Friday
19

○ FULL MOON

Record Store Day
Passover Begins

Saturday
20

♉ TAURUS SEASON

Easter Sunday

Sunday
21

CLEAR YOUR MIND

FEELING GOOD ABOUT:	COMING UP NEXT:
NEED TO WORK ON:	

APRIL

Monday
22

Earth Day

Tuesday
23

PASS THIS ON

Wednesday
24

Thursday
25

National Mani-Pedi Day

Friday
26

Independent Bookstore Day

Saturday
27

Sunday
28

GO THE ~~Fuck~~ OUTSIDE

FEELING GOOD ABOUT:	COMING UP NEXT:
NEED TO WORK ON:	

APRIL

Monday
29

Tuesday   Email Debt Forgiveness Day
30

Wednesday   Asian Pacific Islander American Heritage Month
1   Lei Day (Hawaii)

Thursday
2

TELL HER YOU LOVE HER

MAY

SUNDAY	MONDAY	TUESDAY	WEDNESDAY	THURSDAY	FRIDAY	SATURDAY
			1	2	3	4
5	6	7	8	9	10	11
12	13	14	15	16	17	18
19	20	21	22	23	24	25
26	27	28	29	30	31	

PERSONAL GOALS FOR THE MONTH AHEAD:

___

EXCITING ~~SHIT~~ HAPPENING SOON TO PREPARE FOR:

___

DON'T FORGET:

___

THAT THING I DIDN'T ACTUALLY GET DONE:

___

ONE POSITIVE THOUGHT:

___

MAY

Friday
3

YOU DESERVE IT

Kentucky Derby

Saturday
4

● NEW MOON

Cinco De Mayo

Sunday
5

FEELING GOOD ABOUT:	COMING UP NEXT:
NEED TO WORK ON:	

MAY

Monday
6
Ramadan Begins

Tuesday
7

NOBODY NOTICED IT'S OK

Wednesday
8

Thursday
9
Children's Mental Health Awareness Day

AT LEAST YOU'RE COOL ON THE INTERNET

Friday
10

Saturday
11

Mother's Day

Sunday
12

WE BELIEVE IN YOU

FEELING GOOD ABOUT:	COMING UP NEXT:
NEED TO WORK ON:	

MAY

Monday
13

HELLO MY NAME IS Please Stop

Tuesday
14

Wednesday
15

YOU'RE STILL ALIVE

Thursday   National Notebook Day
16

Endangered Species Day   **Friday**
17

Saturday
18

O FULL MOON

World Baking Day   **Sunday**
19

IT'S NICE SOMEWHERE

FEELING GOOD ABOUT:	COMING UP NEXT:
NEED TO WORK ON:	

MAY

Monday
20

Cher's Birthday

Tuesday
21

♊ GEMINI SEASON

Wednesday
22

Harvey Milk Day

Thursday
23

BREATH DEEP

Brother's Day   **Friday**
                                                24

International Jazz Day   **Saturday**
                                                25

                                                Sunday
                                                26

THE WORLD IS JUST OKAY

FEELING GOOD ABOUT:	COMING UP NEXT:
NEED TO WORK ON:	

MAY

Monday
27
Memorial Day

Tuesday
28

THINGS DO CHANGE

Wednesday
29

Thursday
30
National Creativity Day

JUNE

SUNDAY	MONDAY	TUESDAY	WEDNESDAY	THURSDAY	FRIDAY	SATURDAY
						1
2	3	4	5	6	7	8
9	10	11	12	13	14	15
16	17	18	19	20	21	22
23	24	25	26	27	28	29
30						

PERSONAL GOALS FOR THE MONTH AHEAD:

EXCITING ~~SHIT~~ HAPPENING SOON TO PREPARE FOR:

DON'T FORGET:

THAT THING I DIDN'T ACTUALLY GET DONE:

ONE POSITIVE THOUGHT:

JUNE

Friday
31

LGBTQ+ Pride Month

Saturday
1

HAPPINESS IS AN ART

National Cancer Survivors Day

Sunday
2

FEELING GOOD ABOUT:	COMING UP NEXT:
NEED TO WORK ON:	

JUNE

Monday
3

SMART FOR IDIOTS

● NEW MOON

Tuesday
4

Wednesday   Eid al-Fitr (Ramadan Ends)
5

Thursday
6

OPEN UP A LITTLE

National Doughnut Day **Friday**
7

Best Friends Day **Saturday**
8

JUST WAIT A MINUTE

Sunday
9

FEELING GOOD ABOUT:

NEED TO WORK ON:

COMING UP NEXT:

JUNE

Monday
10

(IDK)

Tuesday   Kamehameha Day (Hawaii)
11

Wednesday
12

Thursday
13

YOU STILL HAVE TO SHOW UP

Flag Day

Friday
14

Saturday
15

Father's Day

Sunday
16

SEE YOU NEXT TIME

FEELING GOOD ABOUT:	COMING UP NEXT:
NEED TO WORK ON:	

JUNE

Monday
17

○ FULL MOON

Tuesday
18

YOU'RE SOMEBODY'S WORLD

Wednesday   Juneteenth
19

Thursday
20

PUT A SECRET HERE & FOLD IT UP

IF AT FIRST YOU
DON'T SUCCEED...

CONGRATULATIONS
WELCOME TO LIFE
IT IS HARD SOME-
TIMES BUT ALSO
MOSTLY OKAY

LIST YOUR CURRENT GOALS & LET'S MANIFEST THIS ~~SHIT~~!!!

[COMPLETE LYRICS TO ABBA'S "GIMME! GIMME! GIMME! (A MAN AFTER MIDNIGHT)"]

JUNE

First Day of Summer

Friday
21

♋ CANCER SEASON

National Onion Rings Day

Saturday
22

Sunday
23

EAT SOMETHING?

FEELING GOOD ABOUT:	COMING UP NEXT:
NEED TO WORK ON:	

JUNE

Monday
24

I KNOW THAT'S RIGHT

Tuesday
25

Wednesday   Tropical Cocktails Day
26

Thursday   National HIV Testing Day
27

EMBRACE BREATHING

Friday
28

National Camera Day

Saturday
29

Sunday
30

SUNLIGHT DOES HELP

FEELING GOOD ABOUT:	COMING UP NEXT:
NEED TO WORK ON:	

July

Monday
1

Canada Day

FIND YOUR WAY BACK

Tuesday
2

Michelle Branch's Birthday

● *NEW MOON*

Wednesday
3

Thursday
4

Independence Day (USA)

JULY

SUNDAY	MONDAY	TUESDAY	WEDNESDAY	THURSDAY	FRIDAY	SATURDAY
	1	2	3	4	5	6
7	8	9	10	11	12	13
14	15	16	17	18	19	20
21	22	23	24	25	26	27
28	29	30	31			

PERSONAL GOALS FOR THE MONTH AHEAD:

___

___

___

EXCITING ~~SHIT~~ HAPPENING SOON TO PREPARE FOR:

___

___

___

DON'T FORGET:

___

___

THAT THING I DIDN'T ACTUALLY GET DONE:

___

ONE POSITIVE THOUGHT:

___

JULY

Comic Sans Day

Friday
5

International Kissing Day

Saturday
6

MAKE A PLAN

Sunday
7

☆ MERCURY RETROGRADE BEGINS

FEELING GOOD ABOUT:	COMING UP NEXT:
NEED TO WORK ON:	

JULY

Monday
8

Tuesday   Cow Appreciation Day
9

Wednesday
10

SENTIMENTALIZE!

Thursday   Free Slurpee® Day
11

THE UNKNOWN

Friday
12

YOU ARE APPRECIATED

Saturday
13

Sunday
14

FEELING GOOD ABOUT:	COMING UP NEXT:
NEED TO WORK ON:	

JULY

Monday
15

Tuesday — National Fresh Spinach Day
16

O FULL MOON

Wednesday — National Hot Dog Day
17

GO OUTSIDE

Thursday
18

YOUTU.BE/qoUqvxSx4bU

Friday
19

Saturday
20

CREATE A PERIMETER

National Ice Cream Day

Sunday
21

FEELING GOOD ABOUT:	COMING UP NEXT:
NEED TO WORK ON:	

JULY

Monday
22

OUT OF OFFICE

Tuesday   Gorgeous Grandma Day
23

♌ LEO SEASON

Wednesday
24

Thursday
25

GET SOME REST PLEASE

National Talk In An Elevator Day

Friday
26

Saturday
27

Parents' Day

Sunday
28

WISDOM IS A GIFT

FEELING GOOD ABOUT:	COMING UP NEXT:
NEED TO WORK ON:	

JULY

Monday
29

Tuesday　　　　　　　　　　International Day of Friendship
30

Wednesday
31

● NEW MOON
★ MERCURY RETROGRADE ENDS

Thursday
1

THANK YOURSELF

AUGUST

SUNDAY	MONDAY	TUESDAY	WEDNESDAY	THURSDAY	FRIDAY	SATURDAY
				1	2	3
4	5	6	7	8	9	10
11	12	13	14	15	16	17
18	19	20	21	22	23	24
25	26	27	28	29	30	31

PERSONAL GOALS FOR THE MONTH AHEAD:

EXCITING ~~SHIT~~ HAPPENING SOON TO PREPARE FOR:

DON'T FORGET:

THAT THING I DIDN'T ACTUALLY GET DONE:

ONE POSITIVE THOUGHT:

AUGUST

Friday
2

Saturday
3

ENJOY YOURSELF

Sister's Day
Sunday
4

FEELING GOOD ABOUT:	COMING UP NEXT:
NEED TO WORK ON:	

AUGUST

Monday International Assistance Dog Week
5

Tuesday National Gossip Day (but you didn't hear it from me)
6

Wednesday
7

Thursday
8

WE ARE DOING IT

YOU TRIED

Friday
9

National Lazy Day

Saturday
10

Sunday
11

EVERYONE GETS SAD

FEELING GOOD ABOUT:	COMING UP NEXT:
NEED TO WORK ON:	

AUGUST

Monday
12

Tuesday   International Left Handers Day
13

Wednesday
14

SIT UP STRAIGHT

Thursday   National Failures Day
15

O FULL MOON

RELAX

Friday
16

IT'S NOBODY'S "FAULT"

Saturday
17

Sunday
18

FEELING GOOD ABOUT:	COMING UP NEXT:
NEED TO WORK ON:	

AUGUST

Monday
19

National Potato Day

Tuesday
20

Wednesday
21

Thursday
22

MAGIC IS OUT THERE

LIST SIX PEOPLE YOU HAVEN'T SEEN IN KIND OF A WHILE...

NAME

NAME

NAME

NAME

NAME

NAME

DRAW A MAP OF YOUR INSECURITY
(BUT MAYBE NOT TO SCALE FOR
THE SAKE OF SELF-PRESERVATION)

CONGRA-
TULATIONS!

YOU ARE
VISITOR #

00008

TO THIS
PAGE !!!

CLICK HERE NOW

> COVER THIS PAGE IN STARS
> THAT WOULD BE SO NICE!!!

AUGUST

Friday
23

♍ VIRGO SEASON

National Knife Day

Saturday
24

National Banana Split Day

Sunday
25

THERE IS STRENGTH

FEELING GOOD ABOUT:	COMING UP NEXT:
NEED TO WORK ON:	

AUGUST

Monday Women's Equality Day
26

Tuesday
27

Wednesday
28

YOU ARE HONESTLY FINE

Thursday
29

SEPTEMBER

SUNDAY	MONDAY	TUESDAY	WEDNESDAY	THURSDAY	FRIDAY	SATURDAY
1	2	3	4	5	6	7
8	9	10	11	12	13	14
15	16	17	18	19	20	21
22	23	24	25	26	27	28
29	30					

PERSONAL GOALS FOR THE MONTH AHEAD:

_____

_____

_____

EXCITING ~~SHIT~~ HAPPENING SOON TO PREPARE FOR:

_____

_____

_____

DON'T FORGET:

_____

_____

THAT THING I DIDN'T ACTUALLY GET DONE:

_____

ONE POSITIVE THOUGHT:

_____

SEPTEMBER

Friday
30

● NEW MOON

Saturday
31

EMBRACE EMOTION

Sunday
1

FEELING GOOD ABOUT:	COMING UP NEXT:
NEED TO WORK ON:	

SEPTEMBER

Monday
2

Labor Day

Tuesday
3

Wednesday
4

ACKNOWLEDGE YOUR DARKNESS

Thursday
5

National Be Late For Something Day

Friday
6

Saturday
7

HAVE A DRINK

National Grandparents Day   **Sunday**
8

FEELING GOOD ABOUT:	COMING UP NEXT:
NEED TO WORK ON:	

SEPTEMBER

Monday
9

Tuesday World Suicide Prevention Day
10

Wednesday
11

Thursday
12

PERFECT ISN'T BETTER

Friday
13

KNOWING ISN'T FEELING

Saturday
14

○ FULL MOON

Hispanic Heritage Month (Sep. 15 – Oct. 15)   **Sunday**
15

FEELING GOOD ABOUT:	COMING UP NEXT:
NEED TO WORK ON:	

SEPTEMBER

Monday
16
Independence Day (Mexico)

Tuesday
17

Wednesday
18
National Respect Day

RESPECT YOUR PROCESS

Thursday
19

| FPO |

Friday
20

International Day of Peace

Saturday
21

THINK ABOUT IT

Sunday
22

FEELING GOOD ABOUT:	COMING UP NEXT:
NEED TO WORK ON:	

SEPTEMBER

Monday
23

Bi Visibility Day

♎ LIBRA SEASON

Tuesday
24

Wednesday
25

National Comic Book Day

Thursday
26

YOU DON'T KNOW EVERYTHING

NOTE TO SELF

Friday
27

Ask a Stupid Question Day

Saturday
28

● NEW MOON

Sunday
29

GO BE ALONE

FEELING GOOD ABOUT:	COMING UP NEXT:
NEED TO WORK ON:	

OCTOBER

Monday
30
Rosh Hashana (Jewish New Year)

Tuesday
1
First Day of Halloween Month (Basically)

Wednesday
2

TRY AGAIN TOMORROW

Thursday
3
Mean Girls Day (it's October 3rd)

OCTOBER

SUNDAY	MONDAY	TUESDAY	WEDNESDAY	THURSDAY	FRIDAY	SATURDAY
		1	2	3	4	5
6	7	8	9	10	11	12
13	14	15	16	17	18	19
20	21	22	23	24	25	26
27	28	29	30	31		

PERSONAL GOALS FOR THE MONTH AHEAD:

___

EXCITING ~~SHIT~~ HAPPENING SOON TO PREPARE FOR:

___

DON'T FORGET:

___

THAT THING I DIDN'T ACTUALLY GET DONE:

___

ONE POSITIVE THOUGHT:

___

OCTOBER

Cinnamon Roll Day

Friday
4

Saturday
5

JUST WALK AWAY

Sunday
6

FEELING GOOD ABOUT:	COMING UP NEXT:
NEED TO WORK ON:	

OCTOBER

Monday
7
National Flower Day

YOU'RE WORTH IT

Tuesday
8

Wednesday
9
National Take Your Teddy Bear To Work Day

Thursday
10

WHAT HAVE YOU MADE RECENTLY?
SHARE WITH #UA2019HUMBLEBRAG

OK YES
SOME PEOPLE
REALLY DON'T
CARE BUT BY
DEFINITION
EVERYONE
ELSE DOES!!!

DOUBLE TAP THIS PAGE
...TO DO NOTHING

FREE ADVICE:

- DON'T BE RACIST
- DON'T BE SEXIST
- DON'T BE CLASSIST
- DON'T BE HOMOPHOBIC
- DON'T BE ABLEIST
- LET PEOPLE LIVE
- THANK YOU

OCTOBER

National Coming Out Day **Friday**
World Egg Day **11**

International Moment of Frustration Scream Day **Saturday**
12

BE PATIENT

National No Bra Day **Sunday**
13

○ FULL MOON

FEELING GOOD ABOUT:	COMING UP NEXT:
NEED TO WORK ON:	

OCTOBER

Monday
14
Indigenous Peoples' Day

Tuesday
15

SUPPORT YOURSELF

Wednesday
16

Thursday
17
Black Poetry Day

Friday
18

Adam J. Kurtz's Birthday

Saturday
19

TAKE A NAP

Sunday
20

FEELING GOOD ABOUT:	COMING UP NEXT:
NEED TO WORK ON:	

OCTOBER

Monday   Apple Day
21

Tuesday
22

Wednesday
23

♏ SCORPIO SEASON (GOOD LUCK LMAO)

Thursday
24

FIND A TREE

Friday
25

Saturday
26

PROTECT YOUR INVESTMENTS

Diwali (Hindu New Year)

Sunday
27

● NEW MOON

FEELING GOOD ABOUT:	COMING UP NEXT:
NEED TO WORK ON:	

OCTOBER

Monday　　　　　　　　　　　　　　　　　　International Animation Day
28

Tuesday
29

YOU DO HAVE A BODY

Wednesday
30

Thursday　　　　　　　　　　　　　　　　　　Halloween
31

☆ *MERCURY RETROGRADE BEGINS*

NOVEMBER

SUNDAY	MONDAY	TUESDAY	WEDNESDAY	THURSDAY	FRIDAY	SATURDAY
					1	2
3	4	5	6	7	8	9
10	11	12	13	14	15	16
17	18	19	20	21	22	23
24 / 31	25	26	27	28	29	30

PERSONAL GOALS FOR THE MONTH AHEAD:

___

___

___

EXCITING ~~SHIT~~ HAPPENING SOON TO PREPARE FOR:

___

___

___

DON'T FORGET:

___

___

THAT THING I DIDN'T ACTUALLY GET DONE:

___

ONE POSITIVE THOUGHT:

___

NOVEMBER

Friday
1

Saturday
2

Daylight Savings Time Ends

Sunday
3

YOU ARE OKAY

FEELING GOOD ABOUT:	COMING UP NEXT:
NEED TO WORK ON:	

NOVEMBER

Monday
4

#2 BOSS

Tuesday
5

Wednesday   International Stress Awareness Day
6

STAY OUT OF IT

Thursday
7

National S.T.E.M. Day

Friday
8

Saturday
9

CONTROL IS AN ILLUSION

Sunday
10

FEELING GOOD ABOUT:	COMING UP NEXT:
NEED TO WORK ON:	

NOVEMBER

Monday
11
Veterans Day

Tuesday
12

Wednesday
13
World Kindness Day

TAKE A BREAK

Thursday
14

America Recycles Day

Friday
15

[CANCEL]

Saturday
16

WE ARE BOTH RIGHT HERE

Sunday
17

FEELING GOOD ABOUT:	COMING UP NEXT:
NEED TO WORK ON:	

NOVEMBER

Monday
18

FEEL-
INGS

Tuesday　　　　　　　　　　　International Men's Day (lol sure)
19

○ FULL MOON

Wednesday
20

★ MERCURY RETROGRADE ENDS

Thursday
21

THINGS JUST ARE

International Aura Awareness Day   **Friday**
                                     22

♐ SAGITTARIUS SEASON

Saturday
23

Sunday
24

THIS IS JUST PAPER

FEELING GOOD ABOUT:	COMING UP NEXT:
NEED TO WORK ON:	

NOVEMBER

Monday
25

OF COURSE YOU'RE GOOD ENOUGH

Tuesday
26

● NEW MOON

Wednesday
27

Thursday Thanksgiving Day
28

DECEMBER

SUNDAY	MONDAY	TUESDAY	WEDNESDAY	THURSDAY	FRIDAY	SATURDAY
1	2	3	4	5	6	7
8	9	10	11	12	13	14
15	16	17	18	19	20	21
22	23	24	25	26	27	28
29	30	31				

PERSONAL GOALS FOR THE MONTH AHEAD:

EXCITING ~~SHIT~~ HAPPENING SOON TO PREPARE FOR:

DON'T FORGET:

THAT THING I DIDN'T ACTUALLY GET DONE:

ONE POSITIVE THOUGHT:

DECEMBER

Black Friday

Friday
29

SOME THINGS ARE FREE

Saturday
30

World AIDS Day

Sunday
1

FEELING GOOD ABOUT:

NEED TO WORK ON:

COMING UP NEXT:

DECEMBER

Monday　　　　　　　　　　　　　　　　　　　　　　　　　　Cyber Monday
2

Tuesday　　　　　　　　　　International Day of Persons with Disabilities
3　　　　　　　　　　　　　　　　　　　　　　　　　　　Giving Tuesday

Wednesday
4

Thursday
5

DON'T GIVE UP

Friday
6

LET YOURSELF BE

Letter Writing Day   **Saturday**
7

Sunday
8

FEELING GOOD ABOUT:

COMING UP NEXT:

NEED TO WORK ON:

DECEMBER

Monday
9

Tuesday   Human Rights Day
10

YOU ARE A HUMAN BEING

Wednesday
11

Thursday
12

O FULL MOON

ALANIS MORISSETTE
IS A LITERAL GENIUS
SORRY I DON'T MAKE
THE RULES

GO STARE AT YOURSELF IN THE MIRROR FOR A WHILE... GREAT, NOW WHO THE ~~F**k~~ DO YOU THINK YOU ARE???

MAYBE...
YOU SHOULD
HAVE FAITH IN
SOMETHING
INTANGIBLE
JUST IN CASE

WOW I LITERALLY GAVE MYSELF
A BLISTER WRITING THIS
FOR YOU?? IT WAS WORTH IT.

DECEMBER

Friday
13

Saturday
14

NOBODY KNOWS ANYTHING

Sunday
15

FEELING GOOD ABOUT:

NEED TO WORK ON:

COMING UP NEXT:

DECEMBER

Monday
16

National Chocolate Covered Anything Day

Tuesday
17

Wednesday
18

Thursday
19

EAT SOME GREENS

FOR EVER

Friday
20

NEVER GIVING UP IS HOW YOU WIN

First Day of Winter

Saturday
21

Hanukkah Begins

Sunday
22

♑ CAPRICORN SEASON

FEELING GOOD ABOUT:	COMING UP NEXT:
NEED TO WORK ON:	

DECEMBER

Monday
23

BEING LOUDER DOESN'T MAKE YOU RIGHT

Tuesday
24

Wednesday — Christmas Day
25

Thursday — Kwanzaa Begins
26

● *NEW MOON*

[DERIVATIVE
NONSENSE
DRAWING]

Friday
27

Call a Friend Day

Saturday
28

Sunday
29

SMILE MAYBE

FEELING GOOD ABOUT:	COMING UP NEXT:
NEED TO WORK ON:	

DECEMBER

Monday
30

Tuesday New Year's Eve
31

Wednesday New Year's Day 2020
1

GO FOR A WALK

Thursday
2

HAPPY NEW YEAR!

ONE NICE THING ABOUT THE WORLD ENDING IS THAT I'LL FINALLY BE ABLE TO STOP COMPARING MYSELF TO OTHERS :) :) :)

IT'S JUST PAPER!

YOU CAN COMPLAIN
ON HERE & NOBODY'S
GONNA SAY ANYTHING

NEVER FORGET:

- WASH YOUR HANDS
- LOOK BOTH WAYS
- TREAT OTHERS WELL
- EAT VEGETABLES
- SHARE WISDOM
- SMILE AT DOGS
- FEEL THE SUN
- TRY NEW THINGS
- LIFE GOES ON
- THAT 1 THING

Adam J. Kurtz is an artist and author whose illustrative work is rooted in honesty, humor and a little darkness.

His books have been translated into over a dozen languages and his "very personal" work for clients like Strand Bookstore and Urban Outfitters has been featured in the *New Yorker*, VICE, Adweek and more. Visit adamjk.com or @adamjk for more.

Unsolicited Advice is an annual self-published work (since 2011) that is only made possible by your purchase. Thank you for your support of this year's edition. See you next year??

ALSO AVAILABLE FROM ADAM J. KURTZ

- 1 Page AT A TIME
- PICK ME UP
- THINGS ARE WHAT YOU MAKE OF THEM
- WHAT I AM TRYING TO SAY TO YOU (POSTCARDS)
- THEN & NOW UNDATED TWELVE-MONTH AGENDA
- THE OK TAROT
- MORE CUTE ~~SHIT~~ AT SHOP.ADAMJK.COM

Inches

LENGTH
1 mi = 1760 yd = 5280 feet = 1.609 km
1 yd = 3ft, 1 ft = 12 in, 1 in = 2.54cm
1 meter = 1.094 yd = 39.27 in = 100 cm

ODD EIGHTHS TO DECIMALS
1/8 = .125, 3/8 = .375, 5/8 = .625, 7/8 = .875

VOLUME
1 gal = 4 qt = 8 pints = 16 cups = 128 oz
1 lt = 1.05 qt, 1 qt = 0.946 lt, 1 pint = 473 ml
1 cubic ft = 7.48 gal, 1 cubic yd = 27 cubic ft

AREA
1 sq mi = 640 acres, 1 acre = 43560 sq ft
1 sq yd = 9 sq ft, 1 sq ft = 144 sq in

MASS
1 ton = 2000 lb = 907 kg, 1 kg = 2.2 lb
1 oz = 28.35 g, 1 lb = 16 oz = 453.6 g

TEMPERATURE
°C = 5/9(°F - 32), °F = 9/5(°C + 32)
Freezing = 0°C / 32°F & Boiling = 100°C / 212°F

TIPPING
Move decimal point one digit to the left to calculate 10%,
then double (tip for $73.42 becomes $7.35 x 2, or $14.70).
If you can afford to eat out, you can afford to tip fairly. Bon appetit!

KITCHEN CONVERSIONS
3 tsp = 1 tbsp, 4 tbsp = ¼ cup, 5 tbsp + 1 tsp = 1/3 cup
1 tsp = 5 ml, 1 cup = 240 ml, 1 oz = 28 g, 1 lb = 454 g

STANDARD U.S. PAPER SIZES
Letter = 8.5" x 11", Legal = 8.5" x 14", Tabloid = 11" x 17"

DEFAULT ADVICE FOR ALL SITUATIONS
Take some deep breaths. Sit down. Try to drink some water. Get yourself to a place of calm. Try to think objectively and make a decision rooted in rational thought. You can handle this. Every experience you have had up until now has made you uniquely qualified for the next challenge. I believe in you. Really.

Made in the USA
San Bernardino, CA
17 October 2018